IQ WORKOUT

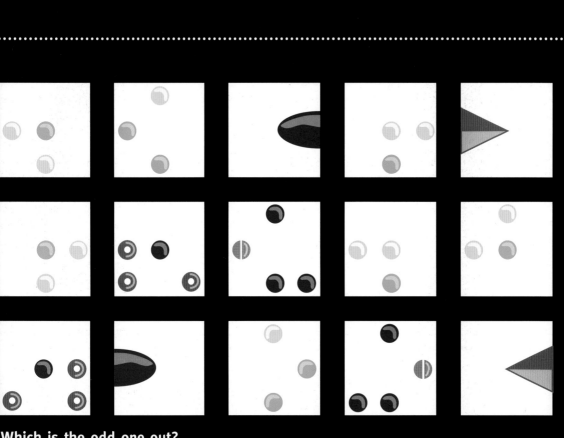

Which is the odd one out?

IQ WORKOUT

**Quick and Effective Exercises
to Boost your Brain Power**

Philip Carter
and
Ken Russell

BARRON'S

Editor: Ulla Weinberg
Copy Editor: Ian Kearey
Art Editors: Francis Cawley, Elizabeth Healey
Designer: Liz Brown
Illustrators: Jennie Dooge, Peter Mundee
Art director: Moira Clinch
QUAR.IYI

Manufactured by
Regent Publishing Services, China
Printed by
Leefung-Asco Printers Ltd, China

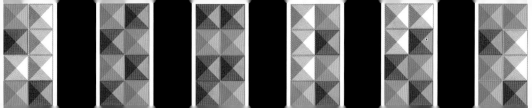

INTRODUCTION

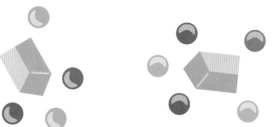

THE HUMAN BRAIN, with an average weight of only 3 lb (1.36 kg), is infinitely more complex than any computer, and is the natural product of hundreds of thousands of years of evolution. This intricate web of nerves somehow manages to regulate all the systems in the body, and at the same time absorbs and learns from a continual intake of the thoughts, feelings and memories. Yet we all have the capacity to put our brain to even more use by exploring new avenues, experiences, and learning adventures.

The use of IQ tests and puzzles can be of immense value in pushing out the boundaries of your brain power beyond what you might think possible. Just as gymnasts will improve their performances and increase their chances of success by means of punishing training schedules and refinement of technique, tests and puzzles can provide you with the mental gymnastics to substantially increase your brain power.

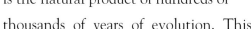

So what exactly is an intelligence, or IQ, test? The letters IQ stand for "Intelligence Quotient." Although intelligence is possessed by all people, it varies in amount, and remains the same throughout your life from approximately 18 years of age. It enables you to deal with real situations and to profit intellectually from sensory experience. Any valid intelligence test will measure adaptive and successful functioning within specific environments, such as reasoning, judging, learning, and dealing with novel situations.

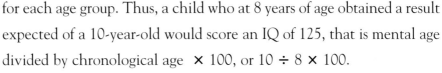

When measuring the IQ of a child, it is given an intelligence test that has already been given to thousands of other children, and an average score has been assessed for each age group. Thus, a child who at 8 years of age obtained a result expected of a 10-year-old would score an IQ of 125, that is mental age divided by chronological age × 100, or 10 ÷ 8 × 100.

With adults, this method of calculation does not apply. Mental age goes through constant development to about the age of 13, and begins to slow up after that. Little or no improvement is found beyond the age of 18. Of course, we all continue to learn throughout life, but the mental ability that enables us to do this does not improve during adulthood. Adults have, therefore, to be judged on an IQ test whose average score is 100, and the results are graded above and below this norm according to known scores.

If adult IQ remains constant throughout life, how can you improve your performance in IQ tests? We believe that by practicing different types of IQ tests, and by getting your mind attuned to the different types of questions you may encounter, it is possible to improve by a few vital percentage points.

IQ tests are set and used on the assumption that when taking the test, you know nothing of the testing method, and very little about the question methods within the tests. Therefore, if you learn about this form of testing and know how to approach the different kinds of questions, you can improve your performance in the tests themselves.

There are many different components of what is commonly understood by the term "intelligence," and all or some of the following will be tested in a typical IQ test: spatial awareness, memory, perception, numerical, verbal, and lexical abilities. In the past, mastery of words was seen as the true measure of intelligence, and vocabulary tests have been widely used in intelligence testing. Today, however, there is a swing towards diagrammatic tests where logic is more important than word knowledge. These tests include a large proportion of spatial questions, such as the one illustrated below.

Which figure continues the sequence?

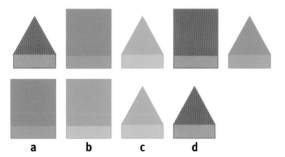

a   b   c   d

The answer in this example is the blue square (b), because the sequence runs triangle, square, triangle, square, etc., while the color sequence runs brown, green, blue, etc.

Advocates of such nonverbal, or culture-neutral, tests argue that diagrammatic tests examine raw intelligence without the influence of prior knowledge. The tests are designed to probe your understanding of spatial relationship and design, and this book devotes Chapters 1 and 4, Amazing Patterns and Visualizing Movement, to this type of test.

All of the puzzles in this book are designed to test your powers of logic and your ability to deal with problems in a structured and analytical way. They are also designed to make you think laterally and creatively; in other words, not to take things at face value but to look beyond the façade in order to seek out a solution. Developing these skills can also prove invaluable in dealing with many real-life problems that you may encounter.

To take another example that explores the thought processes necessary to solve puzzles of a spatial and numerical nature:

What number should replace the question mark?

In this kind of test, it is necessary to allow your mind to freely explore all the various possibilities. Is there any logical progression of the numbers, looking clockwise or counterclockwise around the circle? Does one hemisphere add up to the same as the opposite hemisphere? Is there any reason why all the numbers are different? If you explore enough possibilities, you should discover the logic behind the question and arrive at the correct answer. In this case, look at the opposite segments and you will see that each pair totals 11. It follows, therefore, that the missing number is 6, so that the opposite segments, 6 + 5, total 11.

The examples given here are designed to provide a flavor of the type of question you will encounter as you work through the book.

How to use this book

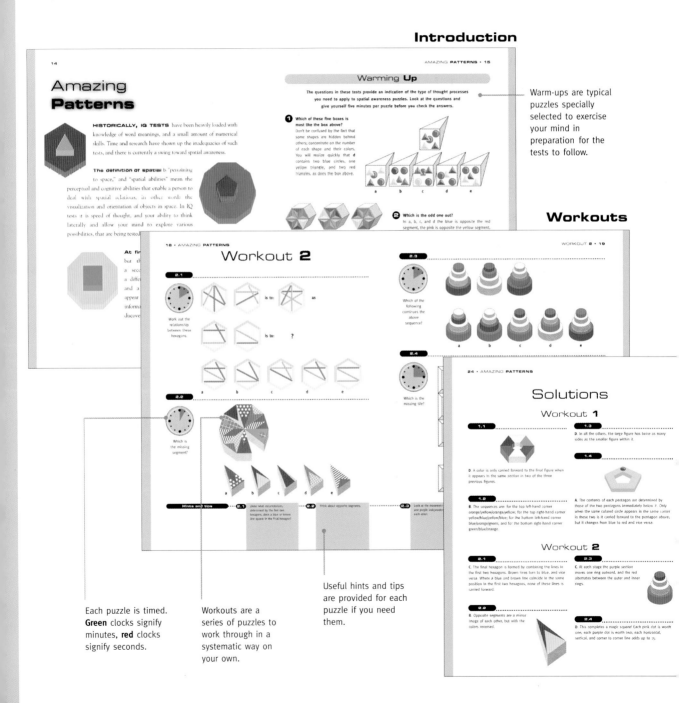

Introduction

Warm-ups are typical puzzles specially selected to exercise your mind in preparation for the tests to follow.

Workouts

Each puzzle is timed. **Green** clocks signify minutes, **red** clocks signify seconds.

Workouts are a series of puzzles to work through in a systematic way on your own.

Useful hints and tips are provided for each puzzle if you need them.

The five chapters of this book are each devoted to a selection of puzzles that test a specific skill in the following areas: nonverbal reasoning, logical thinking, numeracy, spatial perception, and memory. Each chapter contains an introduction, three Warm-up tests, and several Workouts. The warm-up tests present you with typical puzzles selected to exercise your mind in preparation for the tests to follow. They provide an insight into the thought processes behind the puzzles, and we guide you through the working of the puzzles, showing the best way to approach them. This section is followed by Workouts, groups of puzzles to try on your own. Each puzzle is graded according to the time it should take to finish it. Should you have difficulty solving the puzzle in the time allowed, useful hints are provided for each puzzle on the bottom of the page. Solutions, with explanations, appear after every chapter, except in Sharpen Up Your Memory, where you check your answers against the original questions. An assessment is provided with the solutions (except in Sharpen Up Your Memory), which will help you to measure your performance in each of the areas tested in this book.

The second part of the book is comprised of two complete IQ tests, each of 25 questions, that incorporate a selection of the various types of puzzles encountered in the book. A special introduction – Don't Panic – gives useful tips on how to successfully master a typical test situation. Each set of 25 questions is timed, and an assessment of your performance is provided at the end of each set of answers and explanations. *Note*: measurements are not converted; the figures are important, not the measurement system.

Solutions

WORKOUT **SOLUTIONS** • 25

Workout **3**

3.1
...en the same color circle appears in an ellipse, these ...s are replaced by two different color circles at the ...stage.

3.2

...the others have a mirror image pairing.

3.3
B. Looking across and down each line, the contents of the third tile are determined by the contents of the first two tiles. Only when a color appears in the same segment in both the previous squares is it carried forward to the third tile, changing from red to purple, and vice versa.

3.4
B. The square goes into the diamond, having reduced in size, and the diamond rotates through 90°.

Workout **4**

4.1
...s completes every possible pairing of the four ..., red, yellow, green, and blue, that is red/yellow, ...een, red/blue, yellow/green, yellow/blue, and .../blue.

4.2
...tions a and d are the same, but with red and yellow ...ed; the same applies to c and e.

4.3
D. The red line in each box represents a mirror, and only option d shows the correct mirror image.

4.4
E. Each horizontal and vertical line contains heart, spade, and club, and the three colors red, blue, and yellow appear on the three suits and in the background in each line. On each line one of the figures is inverted.

Assessment:
4–6	= Average
7–10	= Good
11–14	= Very good
15–16	= Exceptional

Solutions, with explanations, appear after every chapter.

An assessment of your performance is given at the end of each Workout section.

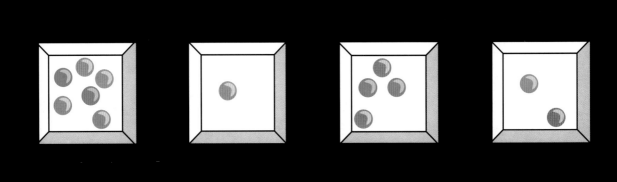

PART 1
THE WORKOUTS

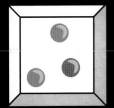 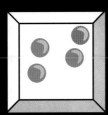 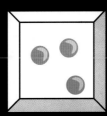 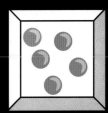

Amazing
Patterns

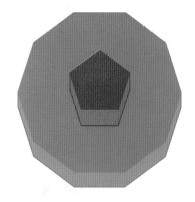

HISTORICALLY, IQ TESTS have been heavily loaded with knowledge of word meanings, and a small amount of numerical skills. Time and research have shown up the inadequacies of such tests, and there is currently a swing toward spatial awareness.

The definition of spatial is "pertaining to space," and "spatial abilities" mean the perceptual and cognitive abilities that enable a person to deal with spatial relations, in other words the visualization and orientation of objects in space. In IQ tests it is speed of thought, and your ability to think laterally and allow your mind to explore various possibilities, that are being tested.

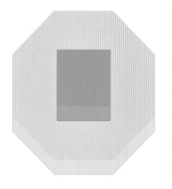

At first sight, such tests may appear daunting, but the trick is never to give up. Often a second look at the problem will reveal a different approach, and a solution will appear because further information has been discovered.

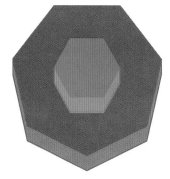

Warming **Up**

The questions in these tests provide an indication of the type of thought processes you need to apply to spatial awareness puzzles. Look at the questions and give yourself five minutes per puzzle before you check the answers.

1 **Which of these five boxes is most like the box above?**

Don't be confused by the fact that some shapes are hidden behind others; concentrate on the number of each shape and their colors. You will realize quickly that **d** contains two blue circles, one yellow triangle, and two red triangles, as does the box above.

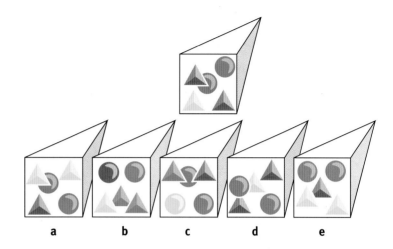

a   b   c   d   e

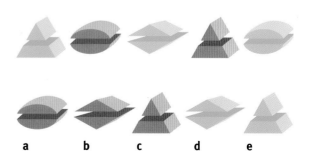

a   b   c
d   e

2 **Which is the odd one out?**

In a, b, c, and d the blue is opposite the red segment, the pink is opposite the yellow segment, and the brown is opposite the green segment. By contrast, **e** contains a yellow opposite a blue segment and a pink opposite a red segment, so it must be the odd one out.

3 **What continues the above sequence?**

You need to split the possible sequences of color and shape, and examine each one in turn before putting them together. The sequence of shapes runs triangle, ellipse, diamond, and is repeated, and the color sequence runs turquoise, orange, and is repeated. The next one should be orange and a diamond, so **b** is the correct answer.

a   b   c   d   e

Workout **1**

Each of the following four workouts comprises four different types
of puzzles that involve similar logical thought processes. Each puzzle is timed,
and hints to solving each one are provided at the bottom of the page, as a last resort.

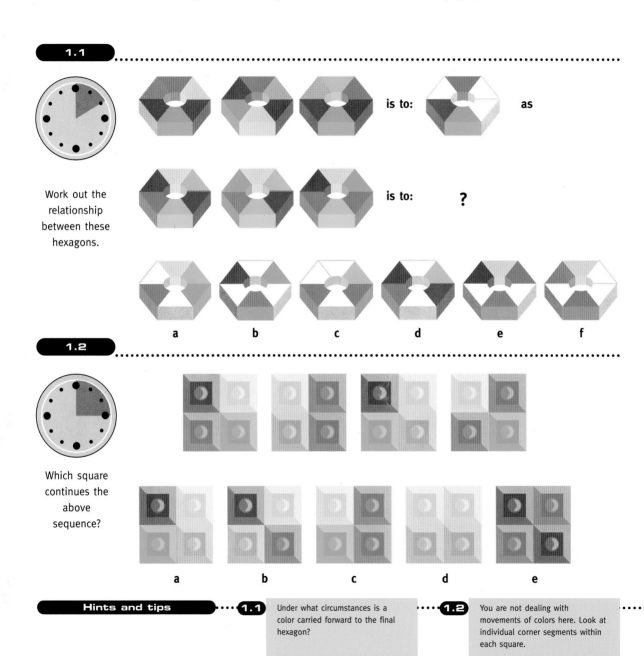

1.1

Work out the
relationship
between these
hexagons.

is to:

as

is to:

?

a   b   c   d   e   f

1.2

Which square
continues the
above
sequence?

a   b   c   d   e

Hints and tips

1.1 Under what circumstances is a
color carried forward to the final
hexagon?

1.2 You are not dealing with
movements of colors here. Look at
individual corner segments within
each square.

1.3

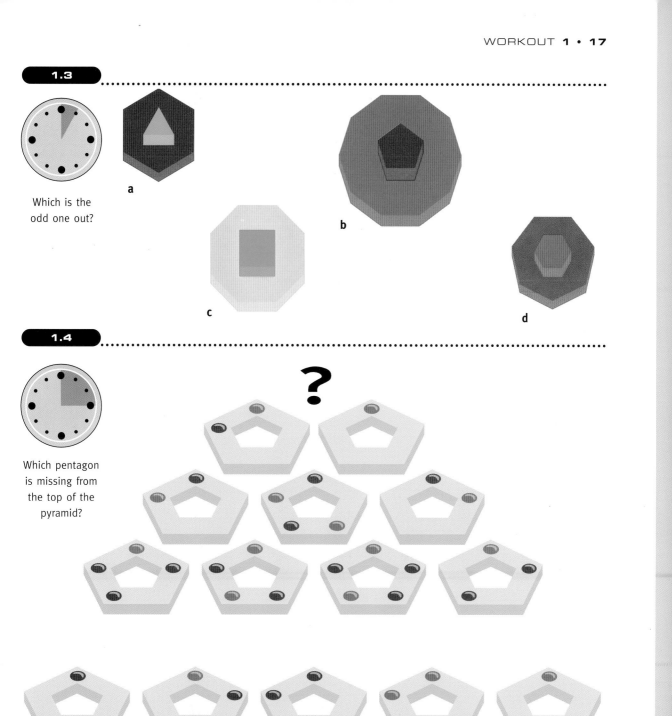

Which is the
odd one out?

a

b

c

d

1.4

?

Which pentagon
is missing from
the top of the
pyramid?

a   b   c   d   e

1.3 Look for a relationship between
each of the larger figures and the
figure contained within it.

1.4 The contents of each pentagon are
determined by the contents of the
two pentagons directly below it.

For solutions see pages 24-5

Workout **2**

2.1

Work out the
relationship
between these
hexagons.

  is to:  **as**

  is to: **?**

a   b   c   d   e

2.2

Which is
the missing
segment?

a   b   c   d   e

Hints and tips

2.1 Under what circumstances, determined by the first two hexagons, does a blue or brown line appear in the final hexagon?

2.2 Think about opposite segments.

2.3

Which of the
following
continues the
above
sequence?

a   b   c   d   e

2.4

Which is the
missing tile?

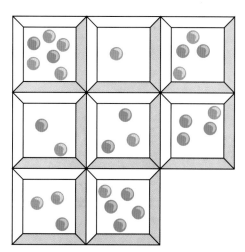

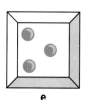

a   b   c   d   e

2.3 Look at the movement of orange and purple independently from each other.

2.4 In a magic number square, each horizontal, vertical, and corner to corner line equals 15. Try allocating value to the colors.

For solutions see pages 24-5

Workout 3

3.1

What comes
next in the
sequence?

    a   b   c   d   e

3.2

Which is the
odd one out?

    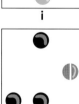 

a   b   c   d   e

f   g   h   i   j

k   l   m   n   o

Hints and tips

3.1 Why do certain colors disappear and others remain in the same position?

3.2 Ignore the colored balls and concentrate on the other shapes. What pattern begins to emerge? Apply this pattern to the balls.

3.3

Which is the
missing tile?

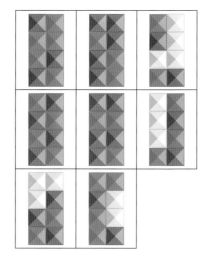

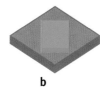

a   b   c   d   e

3.4

Work out the
relationship
between these
shapes.

 is to:  as

 is to: **?**

a   b   c   d   e

3.3 Look at each line across and down, concentrating on the first two squares. When does a certain color appear in the third square?

3.4 Think about change of size and rotation.

For solutions see pages 24-5

Workout **4**

4.1

Which pair
completes the
set?

a   b   c   d   e

4.2

Which is the
odd one out?

 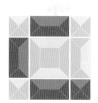

a   b   c

 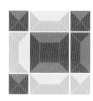

d   e

Hints and tips

4.1 Why must a unique pairing complete the set?

4.2 Think about the way the colors are arranged in each square.

4.3

Which one of
the five boxes
meets the same
conditions as
the box above?

    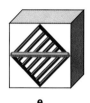

a   b   c   d   e

4.4

Which is the
missing square?

a   b   c   d   e   f

4.3 Why does each box contain a red
line? What might this represent?

4.4 Look along each line and down
each column to find a pattern
occurring.

For solutions see pages 24-5

Solutions

Workout **1**

1.1

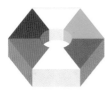

D. A color is only carried forward to the final figure when it appears in the same section in two of the three previous figures.

1.2

B. The sequences are: for the top left-hand corner orange/yellow/orange/yellow; for the top right-hand corner yellow/blue/yellow/blue; for the bottom left-hand corner blue/orange/green; and for the bottom right-hand corner green/blue/orange.

1.3

D. In all the others, the large figure has twice as many sides as the smaller figure within it.

1.4

A. The contents of each pentagon are determined by those of the two pentagons immediately below it. Only when the same colored circle appears in the same corner in these two is it carried forward to the pentagon above; but it changes from blue to red and vice versa.

Workout **2**

2.1

C. The final hexagon is formed by combining the lines in the first two hexagons. Brown lines turn to blue, and vice versa. Where a blue and brown line coincide in the same position in the first two hexagons, none of these lines is carried forward.

2.2

B. Opposite segments are a mirror image of each other, but with the colors reversed.

2.3

C. At each stage the purple section moves one ring outward, and the red alternates between the outer and inner rings.

2.4

D. This completes a magic square! Each pink dot is worth one; each purple dot is worth two; each horizontal, vertical, and corner to corner line adds up to 15.

Workout **3**

3.1

E. When the same color circle appears in an ellipse, these circles are replaced by two different color circles at the next stage.

3.2

J. All the others have a mirror image pairing.

3.3

B. Looking across and down each line, the contents of the third tile are determined by the contents of the first two tiles. Only when a color appears in the same segment in both the previous squares is it carried forward to the third tile, changing from red to purple, and vice versa.

3.4

B. The square goes into the diamond, having reduced in size, and the diamond rotates through 90°.

Workout **4**

4.1

B. This completes every possible pairing of the four colors, red, yellow, green, and blue, that is red/yellow, red/green, red/blue, yellow/green, yellow/blue, and green/blue.

4.2

D. Options a and d are the same, but with red and yellow reversed; the same applies to c and e.

4.3

D. The red line in each box represents a mirror, and only option d shows the correct mirror image.

4.4

E. Each horizontal and vertical line contains heart, spade, and club, and the three colors red, blue, and yellow appear on the three suits and in the background in each line. On each line one of the figures is inverted.

Assessment:

4–6 = Average
7–10 = Good
11–14 = Very good
15–16 = Exceptional

Making Sense of Chaos

THROUGHOUT LIFE we need to be able to restore order from chaos. We need to understand and absorb information quickly, and in these situations the ability to think logically and laterally is of vital importance. In this section the puzzles are designed to encourage you not to take information at face value, but to look beyond the façade to find the solution. If you analyze any problem and successfully find a solution, it is surprising how quickly all the peripheral problems disappear.

Having a logical approach of course only concerns the reasoning process, not the end result. There is no right answer; some solutions may be better than others. A puzzle, however, is set by another person, and has a solution that is already known by that person. The major benefit to be obtained from tackling puzzles is that they stretch and exercise the mind, and enable you to tackle life's problems with renewed vigor and confidence.

Warming **Up**

The questions that follow involve a degree of lateral thinking and logical, analytical approach in order to restore order to the chaos created. Look at the questions and give yourself five minutes per puzzle before you check the answers.

1 **What time should appear on the fourth face?**
In this sequence, the small hand moves back one space at each stage, while the big hand moves forward two spaces at each stage. The correct answer is therefore **e**.

a   b   c   d   e

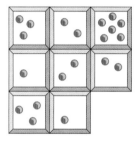

2 **Which is the missing tile?**
Looking across, the number of circles in the third square is the result of multiplying together the numbers of circles in the first two squares. Looking down, the number of circles in the third square is the result of dividing the number of circles in the second square into the number of circles in the first square. Three is the correct number, so **e** is the solution.

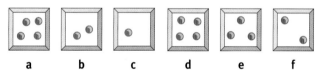

a   b   c   d   e   f

3 **Which is the odd one out?**
Options a and d contain four triangles, and options c and e contain two triangles. Option **b** is the only one to contain three triangles, so it has to be the odd one out.

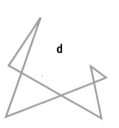

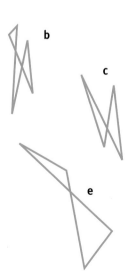

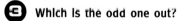

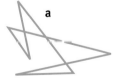

Workout 1

The following four workouts are all culture-neutral and require no particular specialized knowledge. Each of the four puzzles is timed, and hints to solving each one are provided at the bottom of the page if you should need some help.

1.1

What comes next in the sequence?

 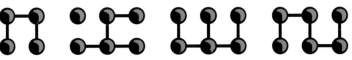

    a   b   c   d   e

1.2

What number should replace the question mark?

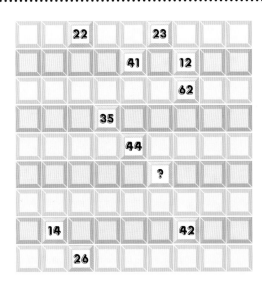

Hints and tips

1.1 View the figures from all angles. Is there anything you can pick out?

1.2 Look across each line and start counting the colored squares in each line. A pattern should begin to emerge.

1.3

Andrea is older than Barbara and Tom. Tom is older than Donna. Bob is younger than Barbara, but older than Donna. Bob is younger than Tom. Andrea is younger than Felicia.

Can you list the group from oldest to youngest?

Andrea

Tom

Barbara

Bob

Felicia

Donna

1.4

What number continues this sequence?

$$11, \quad 23, \quad 58, \quad 1321, \quad 3455, \quad ?$$

1.3 List the first three names downward on some paper. Then slot in the other names according to the information available.

1.4 Try adding the numbers. After the first number 11, how are all subsequent numbers calculated?

For solutions see pages 36-7

Workout **2**

2.1

Which three pieces can be fitted together to form the cube shown on the right?

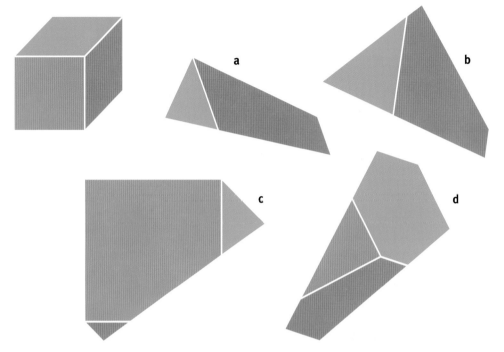

a

b

c

d

2.2

How much money has Mr. Russell lost altogether?

A customer in Russell's shoe store buys a pair of shoes for $40 and pays with a $50 bill. Mr. Russell cannot change the bill, so he asks Mr. Carter at the foodstore next door, who gives him five $10 bills. Mr. Russell returns to his store and gives the customer $10 change. The customer leaves with his shoes and the change. Later Mr. Carter rushes into the shoe store and announces that the $50 bill is counterfeit. Mr. Russell has to give Mr. Carter a real $50 bill, and is unable to apprehend the customer, who has disappeared with the $40 shoes and the $10 bill.

Hints and tips

2.1 Study the colors first. Can you find two pieces that obviously fit together? If so, rotate them and see where the third piece might fit.

2.2 Who has Mr. Russell lost money to in the transaction? Has he lost money to Mr. Carter? Don't forget the value of the shoes.

2.3

Work out which symbol fulfills the criteria.

Which symbol is three to the right of the symbol immediately to the left of the symbol two to the right of the symbol five to the left of the symbol that comes midway between the symbol immediately to the right of the symbol

and the symbol immediately to the left of the symbol ?

2.4

Can you get the mouse into the middle chamber?

This cage consists of 216 chambers. An electronic robot mouse is placed in the top left-hand chamber. With a remote control, it can be moved at each operation either four chambers up or down, and three chambers right or left.

 2.3 Concentrate very hard, and start at the end, working backward.

2.4 Have a close look at the number of chambers. Do you have to think about the mouse's movements to be able to answer the question?

For solutions see pages 36-7

Workout 3

3.1

Work out the relationship between numbers and colored lines.

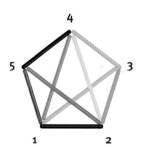

What does this equal?

If  = 115 and  = 172

3.2

Which number fulfills all the criteria?

22	1	2	35	4	34
24	44	48	36	29	12
6	19	5	17	7	23
30	18	8	15	9	14
10	21	3	25	42	11
68	16	13	32	64	20

Which number in the grid is three places away from itself multiplied by 4, two places away from itself plus 2, four places away from itself minus 1, two places away from itself doubled and three places away from itself plus 8?

Hints and tips

3.1 Look from top to bottom and from left to right. What numbers are formed by the colored lines when referred back to the original pentagon? How do these numbers relate to the two examples?

3.2 Which is the highest number divisible by 4? This should lead you to the highest possible number that can be the answer. Then start eliminating numbers.

3.3

Was the car
dealer correct?
If so, how
much did
he lose?

A used-car dealer complained to a friend that he had just had a bad day. "I sold only two cars," he moaned, "for $7500 each. One of the cars gave me 25% profit on outlay, but the other lost 25%."

"That's not so bad," remarked his friend, "at least you broke even."
"No way," said the dealer, "I lost money."

3.4

How many
squares are
there in
this figure?

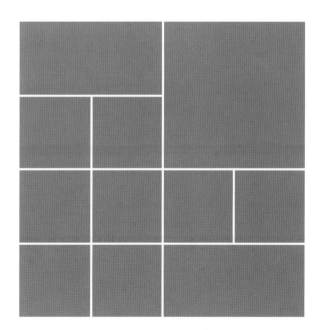

3.3 On $7500 work out how much he would have to pay for a car to make 25%, and how much he would have to pay for a car to lose 25%.

3.4 Try numbering each individual component from 1 to 11.

For solutions see pages 36-7

Workout **4**

4.1

Which number came up the most times?

The manager of the casino wished to check the bias in his roulette wheel, so he asked six of his croupiers to record each spin and let him know which of the numbers 1–36 (excluding zero) came up the most times during one week. These were the answers he received:

A. It was an odd number

B. It was a prime number: 2, 3, 5, 7, 11, 13, 17, 19, 23, 29, 31

C. It was a square number: 1, 4, 9, 16, 25, 36

D. The number had at least one 2 in it

E. The number was either 10, 15, 20, 25, 30 or 35

F. The number was either 28, 29, 30, 32, 33, 34

However, half of the croupiers were not telling the truth.

4.2

Which number is on the opposite face to four on the die?

Three views are shown of a very strange die, which does not contain the usual numbers that you would expect to find on a die.

Each face of the die is a different color but in the puzzle we show just one colored face.

Hints and tips

4.1 Approach the puzzle in a systematic fashion and list all the possibilities.

4.2 You are not looking for the usual pattern where opposite numbers of a die total 7. You may not even be looking for a die that contains the numbers 1–6. Look at the first two views of the die. Do you see anything unusual?

4.3

What numbers should go in the missing spaces?

5	4		6	7	5
8	7	2	7	3	7
3		6	8	6	4
8		8	5	2	7
7	5	1	6	7	4
4	6	8	3		8

4.4

How did Alison know?

Alison Russell bumped into an old college friend. "Hello," she said, "I haven't seen or heard of you since graduation in 1983, what's happened to you?"
"Well," said the friend, "I got married in 1989 to somebody you wouldn't know, and this is my son."
"Hello," said Alison to the boy. "What's your name?" "It's the same as my father's," said the boy. "Ah," said Alison, "so your name must be Peter."

4.3 The numbers appear to have been distributed at random; but have they? Why do some numbers appear in the grid more than others? Are the numbers placed in the grid to any definite rule?

4.4 What information are we given in the puzzle about Alison's friend? If you haven't already solved the puzzle, the assumptions you have made about the friend are not correct.

For solutions see pages 36-7

Solutions

Workout **1**

1.1

D. Rotate the page counterclockwise and look at the figures sideways. The numbers 5, 4, 3, 2 will appear. Option d is the next descending number: 1.

1.2

53. Looking across each line, each number represents the number of consecutive colored squares before it, and the number of consecutive squares after it. The missing number is 53 because there are 5 consecutive orange squares before and 3 consecutive orange squares after it.

1.3

The order of age is: Felicia, Andrea, Barbara, Tom, Bob, and Donna.

1.4

The answer is 89144.

(11) 1 + 1 = 2 + 1 = 3 = 23
(23) 2 + 3 = 5 + 3 = 8 = 58
(58) 5 + 8 = 13 + 8 = 21 = 1321
(1321) 13 + 21 = 34 + 21 = 55 = 3455
(3455) 34 + 55 = 89 + 55 = 144 = 89144

Workout **2**

2.1

The answer is d, a, c.

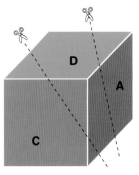

2.2

He loses no money to Mr. Carter, who has given him five $10 bills in exchange for a genuine $50 bill, eventually. All he has lost is the value of the shoes ($40) and the $10 bill he gave the customer as change, a total of $50.

2.3

It is the heart-shaped symbol.

2.4

It is impossible. Because there are 216 chambers, an even number, there is no middle chamber!

Workout **3**

3.1

254. Looking from top to bottom and right and left of each colored line, add up the numbers thus formed, that is $45 + 43 + 51 + 32 + 41 + 42 = 254$.

3.3

The dealer was correct: he has lost money. The car that made him 25% profit cost him $6000, as $6000 + 25% ($1500) = $7500. The car that made him a loss cost him $10,000, as $10,000 − 25% ($2500) = $7500. He therefore lost $2500 − $1500 = $1000.

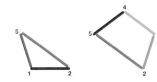

3.2

The answer is 3.

22	1	2	35	4	34
24	44	48	36	29	12
6	19	5	17	7	23
30	18	8	15	9	14
10	21	3	25	42	11
68	16	13	32	64	20

$3 \times 4 = 12$
$3 + 2 = 5$
$3 - 1 = 2$
$3 + 8 = 11$
$3 \times 2 = 6$

3.4

The answer is 14.

One	Three	Four	Eleven
2	1, 2, 3	2, 3, 5, 6	1, 2, 3, 4, 5, 6, 7, 8, 9, 10
3	7, 8, 11	5, 6, 9, 10	
4			
5			
6			
7			
8			
9			
10			

1		4	
2	3		
5	6	7	8
9	10	11	

Workout **4**

4.1

23. Tabulate the six responses. As three of the croupiers had lied, three told the truth. You are, therefore, looking for a number with three ticks.

4.3

5, 6, 8, 8. The grid contains 1×2, 2×2, 3×3, 4×4, 5×5, 6×6, 7×7 and 8×8. All numbers are placed so that the same number is never horizontally or vertically adjacent.

5	4	⑧	6	7	5
8	7	2	7	3	7
3	⑧	6	8	6	4
8	⑥	8	5	2	7
7	5	1	6	7	4
4	6	8	3	⑤	8

4.2

6. This particular die contains two sixes but no five. The 6 is not the same 6 in view 1 as in view 2: the 2 is sloping differently if you twist the die around to line up the 6. The numbers on the die are 6, 6, 4, 3, 2, 1 as illustrated in this flattened out version.

4.4

The friend is male and is named Peter.

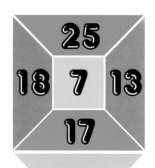

Thinking with
Numbers

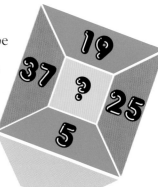

NUMBERS CAN BE CHALLENGING, fascinating, confusing, and frustrating, but once you have developed an interest in them, a whole new world is opened up as you discover their many characteristics and patterns. We all require some numerical skills in our lives, whether it is to calculate our weekly shopping bill or to budget how to use our monthly income. The puzzles here are designed to develop these skills. Anyone who has ever taken an IQ test will be familiar with the type of test encountered, and the more one practices these little puzzles, the more proficient one becomes at solving them.

Take, for example, the simplest of sequences: 2, 4, 6, 8, 10, ? Obviously the answer is 12, because this is a sequence of consecutive even numbers. Now look at this sequence: 2, 4, 6, 10, 16, 26, ? Again there is a series of even numbers starting 2, 4, 6, but then something different happens. The answer is 42 because each subsequent number is the sum of the previous two, that is 6 + 10 = 16, 10 + 16 = 26, therefore 16 + 26 = 42.

Of course, we cannot possibly cover every single type of puzzle that may be encountered in IQ tests, but we can prepare you for the ways in which such brainteasers are presented, and the thought processes you need to apply.

Warming **Up**

Now for a few examples of the type of number puzzles you might encounter in IQ tests,
and the type of thinking needed to solve them. Look at the questions and give yourself five minutes
for each puzzle before looking at the answers.

1 **What number should replace
the question mark?**

You are looking for a common relationship in the
first two pyramids that can equally be applied to
the third pyramid. In this case the common link
is that if you take the difference between the
bottom two numbers, then divide by 2, you arrive
at the number at the top, thus $33 - 19 = 14$, and
$14 \div 2 = 7$, which is the correct answer.

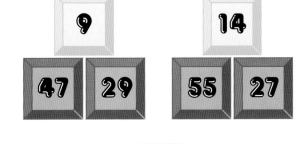

0 , 0 , 1 , 3 , 2 ,
6 , 3 , 9 , 4 , ?

2 **What comes next in the sequence?**

In what seems to be a single sequence there are,
in fact, two separate sequences. The first, starting
with the first 0, simply goes 0, 1, 2, 3, 4, etc., and
the second, starting with the second 0, goes 0, 3,
6, 9, 12, etc., so the answer is **12**.

3 **Which set of numbers below has the same
relationship as the numbers above?**

In the top sequence, the relationship between the
numbers is that the first digit of each number
increases by 2, the second digit reduces by 2, the
third digit increases by 2 and the fourth reduces
by 2. Apply this to each of the alternatives, and
the only one that fits the description is where
2 (+ 2) 9 (− 2) 4 (+ 2) 7 (− 2) = 4765, and
4 (+ 2) 7 (− 2) 6 (+ 2) 5 (− 2) = 6583, so the
correct answer is **a**.

3 7 5 6 : 5 5 7 4 : 7 3 9 2

a 2 9 4 7 : 4 7 6 5 : 6 5 8 3

b 1 7 6 2 : 3 5 7 1 : 5 3 8 0

c 9 5 7 8 : 9 9 6 3 : 9 9 9 1

d 4 6 5 5 : 5 5 6 4 : 6 4 7 3

e 2 8 1 4 : 4 7 1 2 : 6 5 2 1

Workout **1**

When looking at a puzzle, the answer may hit you immediately. If not, your mind must work harder at exploring the options. In the following five workouts, each section is comprised of different types of number puzzles. Each puzzle is timed, and there are hints to solving them at the bottom of the page.

1.1

Which number should replace the question mark?

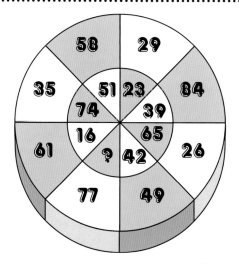

1.2

How much money was shared?

Bill and Al share a certain sum of money in the ratio 4:5. In the end, Al has $60.

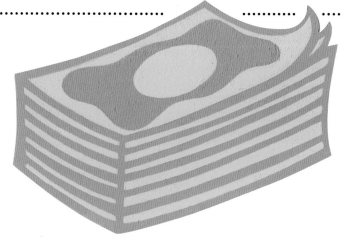

Hints and tips

1.1 Look at the opposite blue and white sections.

1.2 What is the value of each part?

1.3

Which number comes next in the sequence?

1 , 10 , 3 , 8 , 5 ,

6 , 7 , 4 , 9 , ?

1.4

How many matches in total were played before the winner was presented with his trophy?

At the local tennis club 41 entries were received for the men's singles tournament. Because it was a knockout tournament, there had to be a number of byes and preliminary rounds before the last 32 were reached. Throughout the whole of the tournament all matches were played – in other words, no one received a walkover.

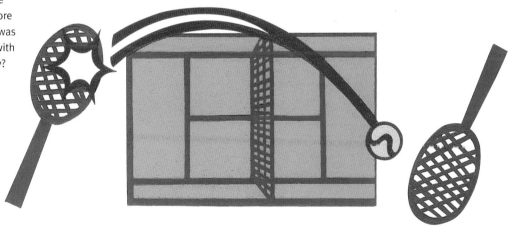

1.3 This is an alternating sequence.

1.4 How many losers were there?

For solutions see pages 50-1

Workout **2**

2.1

For how long did I walk before my wife picked me up?

I finish work each day at 5 P.M. and catch the 5.30 P.M. train that arrives at my hometown station at 6 P.M. My wife drives to the station each day and picks me up at 6 P.M., just as I get off the train. One evening last week, I finished work five minutes early and was able to catch the 5 P.M. train, arriving at my hometown station at 5.30 P.M. Because my wife was not there to collect me, I began to walk home. My wife left home at the usual time, saw me walking home, turned around, picked me up, and drove home. We arrived there 15 minutes earlier than usual.

2.2

What number continues this sequence?

1, 3, 8,

19, 42, ?

Hints and tips

2.1 Think about the total time saved.

2.2 This is both a multiplication and addition sequence, but it is a progressive sequence, the progression being from number to number.

2.3

What number should replace the question mark?

2.4

Which set has the same relationship as the above series of numbers?

19 : 132 : 923

a   25 : 174 : 1217

b   18 : 34 : 66

c   23 : 161 : 1127

d   12 : 73 : 433

e   2 : 18 : 54

2.3 In each circle, look at the numbers in the same color segments and apply the same rule each time to arrive at the third number.

2.4 Try dividing the first number into the second number and then the second number into the third number.

For solutions see pages 50-1

Workout **3**

3.1

What number should replace the question mark?

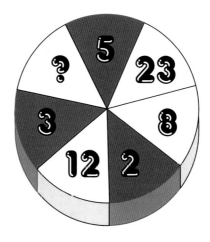

3.2

What number should replace the question mark?

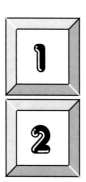

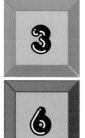

Hints and tips

3.1 Look at the link between the numbers in the red segments.

3.2 Find how the numbers in the blue squares are arrived at. How is this different from the numbers in the red squares?

3.3

What is
the jogger's
average speed?

A man jogs at 6 mph (treat as kmph) over a certain journey and walks back over the same route at 4 mph.

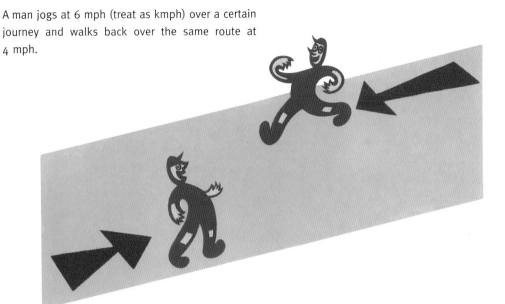

3.4

What number
should replace
the question
mark?

36   (654)   29

72   (5618)   89

84   (?)   22

•••• **3.3** How long does it take to complete a whole journey?   •••• **3.4** How do the numbers in the bracket relate to individual numbers outside the bracket?   **For solutions see pages 50-1** ••••••

Workout **4**

4.1

What number
continues the
sequence?

100, 99, 97,

93, 85, ?

4.2

What number
should replace
the question
mark?

Hints and tips

4.1 Look for a progressive sequence by which the numbers are reducing.

4.2 How do the numbers relate to their position in the grid?

4.3

Which set of numbers below has the same relationship as the two examples above?

18 : 9 : 10

54 : 18 : 15

a 24 : 6 : 20

b 20 : 10 : 18

c 26 : 13 : 15

d 25 : 12 : 16

4.4

What number should replace the question mark?

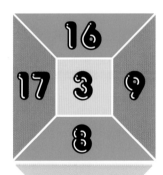

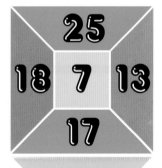

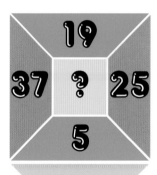

4.3 In each group of three numbers, how is the last number related to the first two?

4.4 In each square, look at the relationship of the numbers in the brown and green segments to the number in the yellow inner square.

For solutions see pages 50-1

Workout **5**

5.1

What number
continues the
sequence?

$$1, \quad 4, \quad 1 1,$$

$$3 4, \quad 1 0 1, \quad ?$$

5.2

What number
should replace
the question
mark?

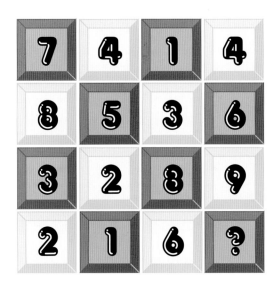

Hints and tips

5.1 This is a progressive sequence that involves multiplication, addition, and subtraction.

5.2 Why are alternate squares colored the same?

5.3

How long does the train take?

A train traveling at a speed of 40 mph (treat as kmph) enters a tunnel that is 1¼ miles (treat as km) long. The length of the train is ¼ mile (km). Work out how long the train needs to pass through the tunnel, from the moment the front enters to the moment the rear emerges.

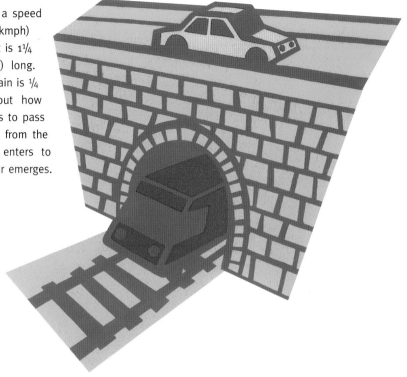

5.4

What number is missing in the sequence?

1 2 4 , 8 1 6 , 3 2 6 ,

? , 8 2 5

5.3 Bear in mind the length of the train plus the length of the tunnel.

5.4 Think of a very familiar sequence in disguise.

For solutions see pages 50-1

Solutions

Workout **1**

1.1

71. The opposing red and yellow segments add up to 100 every time.

1.2

$108. Al's share is $60 = 5 parts, so each part is $12 (60 ÷ 5). The original amount was $12 × 9 = $108.

1.3

2. The first sequence starts at 1 and runs 1, 3, 5, 7, 9, that is + 2 each time. The second sequence starts at 10 and runs 10, 8, 6, 4 2, that is − 2 each time.

1.4

40. This is solved by pure logic. If there are 41 entries, there is only one winner of the tournament. Therefore, during the course of the competition there must be 40 losers. For there to be 40 losers there must be 40 matches in all.

Workout **2**

2.1

22¹/₂ minutes. My wife left at the usual time, so it was before 6 P.M. when she picked me up. As we had saved 15 minutes, that was the time it took her to drive from the point where she picked me up to the station, and back to the same point. If it takes 7¹/₂ minutes each way, my wife picked me up 7¹/₂ minutes before she would normally have picked me up, that is 7¹/₂ minutes before 6 P.M. Therefore I walked for 30 − 7¹/₂ = 22¹/₂ minutes.

2.2

89. Double the previous number and add 1, then 2, then 3 etc.: 1 + 1 + 1 = 3, 3 + 3 + 2 = 8, 8 + 8 + 3 = 19, 19 + 19 + 4 = 42, 42 + 42 + 5 = 89.

2.3

18. Multiply the bottom two numbers together and then divide by 2: (9 × 4) ÷ 2 = 18.

2.4

A (25 : 174 : 1217). Multiply the first number by 7, then deduct 1 to arrive at the second number. Do the same to the second number to arrive at the third number.

Workout **3**

3.1

17. Start at 2 and jump to alternate segments, adding 1, 2, 3, 4, 5, 6.

3.2

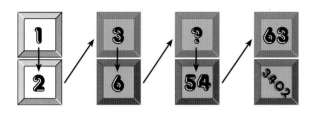

9. The sequence progresses in the direction of the arrows. The numbers in the blue squares are arrived at by adding the two previous numbers, and the numbers in the red squares by multiplying the two previous numbers.

3.3

4.8 mph (treat as kmph). For a journey of 6 miles (treat as km) each way, the outward jog at 6 mph (kmph) would take 1 hour, and the inward walk at 4 mph (kmph) 1.5 hours. Therefore it takes 2.5 hours to travel the total journey of 12 miles (km), or 1 hour for 4.8 miles (km) ($12 \div 2.5$), that is an average speed of 4.8 mph (kmph).

3.4

168.

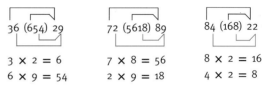

$$3 \times 2 = 6 \qquad 7 \times 8 = 56 \qquad 8 \times 2 = 16$$
$$6 \times 9 = 54 \qquad 2 \times 9 = 18 \qquad 4 \times 2 = 8$$

Workout **4**

4.1

69. The amount being deducted doubles each time: 1, 2, 4, 8 and 16, and $85 - 16 = 69$.

4.2

53. Each number describes its position in the grid. For example, 14 is the first line, fourth column, 53 is the fifth line, third column.

4.3

A (24 : 6 : 20). Divide the first number by the second number, then multiply by 5 to arrive at the third number: $24 \div 6 = 4$ and $4 \times 5 = 20$.

4.4

2. Add the numbers in the green segments, then divide by the difference of the numbers in the brown segments: $(19 + 5) \div (37 - 25) = 24 \div 12 = 2$.

Workout **5**

5.1

304. The sequence runs $\times 3 + 1$, $\times 3 - 1$, so $101 \times 3 + 1 = 304$.

5.2

7. In each line, both across and down, the sums of alternate segments are equal. For example, line 1 across, $7 + 1 = 4 + 4$, line 1 down, $7 + 3 = 8 + 2$.

5.3

2 minutes, 15 seconds. The length of the tunnel plus the train is $1\frac{1}{2}$ miles (treat as km): $1\frac{1}{4}$ tunnel $+ \frac{1}{4}$ train. At a speed of 40 mph (treat as kmph), the train takes $1\frac{1}{2} \times \frac{60}{40}$ minutes to pass through the tunnel, that is $2\frac{1}{4}$ minutes or 2 minutes, 15 seconds.

5.4

412. The number sequence is 1, 2, 4, 8, 16, 32, 64, 128, 256, arranged in groups of 3: 124, 816, 326, 412, 825.

Assessment:

4–6 = Average
7–10 = Good
11–14 = Very good
15–16 = Exceptional

Visualizing
Movement

THE ABILITY TO VISUALIZE movement and manipulate objects in space is called "spatial awareness." Visualization skills can be improved by practicing specific spatial puzzles – a series of geometric shapes that have to be manipulated in the mind as 3-D objects. To find the solution, you might have to mentally rotate, twist, fold, unfold or reverse a variety of objects. The puzzles also demand the use of logic, analysis, classification and sequencing skills (and a good deal of lateral thinking); they do not require verbal skills or specialized knowledge.

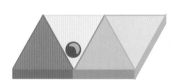

Approach each puzzle separately and calmly, and don't be dazzled by the total effect. As in life, the most obvious answer is often not the correct one, so take time to sort out the hidden workings. Practicing these puzzles can push out the boundaries of your potential and boost your brain power beyond what you may have previously imagined possible.

Warming **Up**

Apart from alertness of mind, what are the thought processes needed to solve spatial awareness puzzles? Work through these examples, and you should begin to get a sense of how they are built up, and the best way to approach them. Study each for five minutes before checking the answers.

❶ Which is the odd one out?
Visualize the shapes being rotated through 360°, and how they will appear at various stages. The odd one out is **c**, because all the others are the same figure rotated, and c has green and blue the other way around from all the rest.

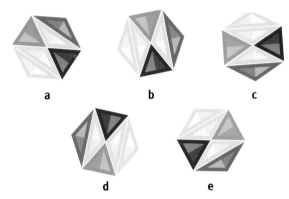

a   b   c

d   e

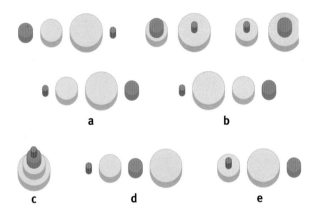

a   b

c   d   e

❷ What comes next in this sequence?
The purple circle is moving from left to right, one circle at a time at each stage. The small red dot is similarly moving from right to left at each stage. The two gray circles remain in the same position throughout. Put the three together, and **a** meets all the requirements.

❸ When the top shape is folded to form a cube, only one of the cubes can be produced. Which one?
When folded. the side with the broad red stripe must be next to the navy blue side with the broad yellow diagonal stripe, and the orange side with the purple cross must then be on top. The correct answer is therefore **d**.

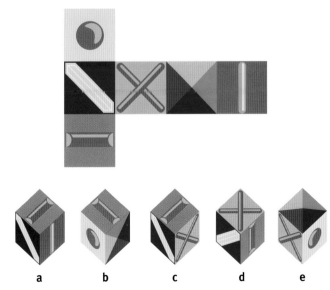

a   b   c   d   e

Workout 1

Now that you have studied the basic principles of spatial puzzles, in the workouts that follow, look at the puzzles and try to solve them within the time limit indicated by the clock. If time is running out, the hints provided may help to put you on the right track.

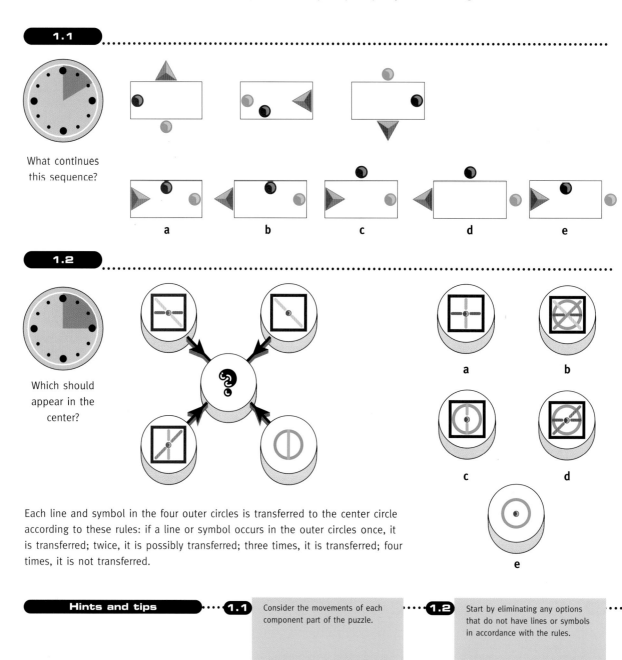

1.1

What continues this sequence?

a   b   c   d   e

1.2

Which should appear in the center?

a   b   c   d

e

Each line and symbol in the four outer circles is transferred to the center circle according to these rules: if a line or symbol occurs in the outer circles once, it is transferred; twice, it is possibly transferred; three times, it is transferred; four times, it is not transferred.

Hints and tips

1.1 Consider the movements of each component part of the puzzle.

1.2 Start by eliminating any options that do not have lines or symbols in accordance with the rules.

1.3

Work out the relationship between these figures.

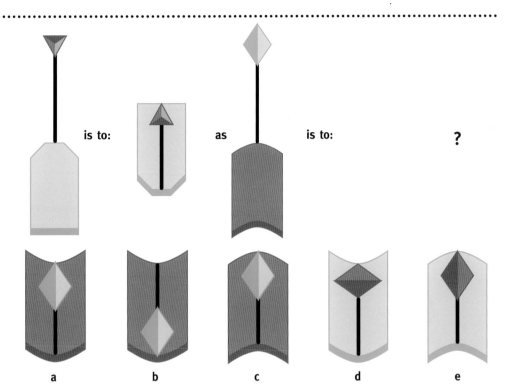

is to: as   is to: ?

    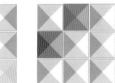

a   b   c   d   e

1.4

Which option continues the sequence?

a   b   c   d   e

1.3 The red and blue portions are folded according to certain rules. Discover these rules in the first example, and you will be able to correctly solve the second example.

1.4 Why does a color disappear off the bottom for one stage, then reappear at the top?

For solutions see pages 64-5

Workout **2**

2.1

What comes
next in the
sequence?

a   b   c   d   e

2.2

Work out the
relationship
between the
circles.

is to:

as

is to: ?

a

b

c

d

e

Hints and tips

2.1 Remember that in this series of
workouts we are visualizing
movement. Work out what in this
puzzle is moving, and how.

2.2 In the first example, how have the
colors changed places? Apply this
same movement to the second
example.

2.3

Which is the
odd one out?

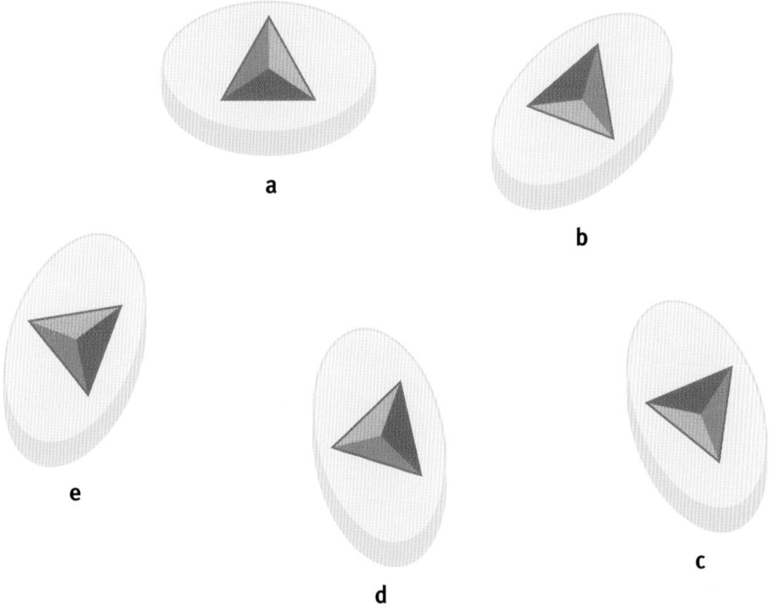

a

b

e

d

c

2.4

What comes
next in the
sequence?

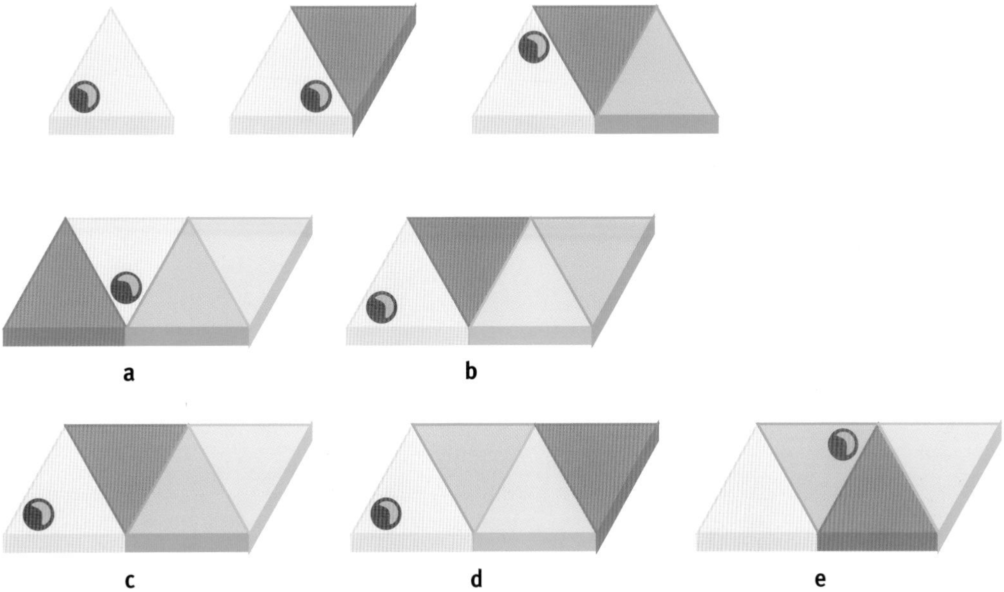

a

b

c

d

e

2.3 Visualize each figure rotated
through 360°, concentrating on the
triangle. Which one is not like the
others?

2.4 Concentrate on the red dot. How is
it moving, and where? How is the
rest of the puzzle being
constructed?

For solutions see pages 64-5

Workout **3**

3.1

What continues
the sequence?

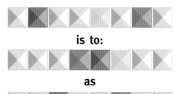

is to:

as

is to: ?

a

b

c

d

e

3.2

What continues
the sequence?

a   b   c   d   e

Hints and tips

3.1 Consider the movement of
individual colors from one stage to
the next.

3.2 Look at the colors in each stack
carefully. Note the differences in
color between each stack. Which
block would you have to move to
create the next stack?

3.3

When the shape
is folded to
form a cube,
just one of the
alternatives can
be produced.
Which one?

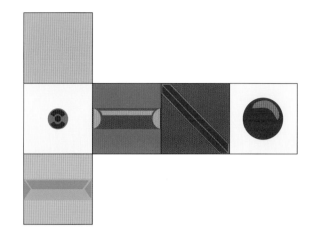

a   **b**   **c**   **d**   **e**

3.4

Work out the
relationship
between these
shapes.

 **is to:**   **as**    **is to: ?**

a   **b**   **c**   **d**   **e**

3.3 Look at the choices available. Try unfolding them in your mind. Note the position of the patterns. Find the correct solution by a process of elimination.

3.4 Work out the relationship between the first two shapes. What rules can you establish? Apply these rules to the second part, and you should find the answer.

For solutions see pages 64-5

Workout **4**

4.1

Work out the relationship between these figures.

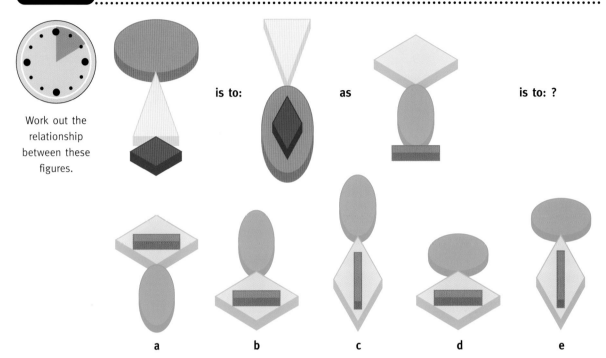

is to: as   is to: ?

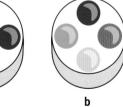

a   b   c   d   e

4.2

What comes next in this sequence?

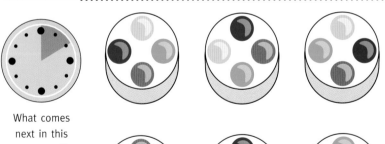

a   b   c   d   e

Hints and tips

4.1 Look at the first example. How have the figures changed? What movement has occurred?

4.2 Analyze the component parts. How is each colored ball moving from stage to stage?

What continues
the sequence?

    a   b   c   d   e

4.4

What continues
the sequence?

    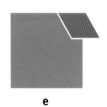

    a   b   c   d   e

4.3 Look at the three arcs individually. How does each change its position from stage to stage?

4.4 Consider the movement of the blue square from stage to stage. Think of the red diamond as a flap attached to the square.

For solutions see pages 64–5

Workout **5**

5.1

What continues
the sequence?

      a   b   c   d   e

5.2

Which hexagon
continues the
sequence?

      a   b   c   d   e

Hints and tips

5.1 Some spatial puzzles require you to visualize a sequence of movements. Look at the balls, and note how they move.

5.2 This puzzle consists of four separate component parts. Each moves in its own individual sequence within the hexagon.

5.3

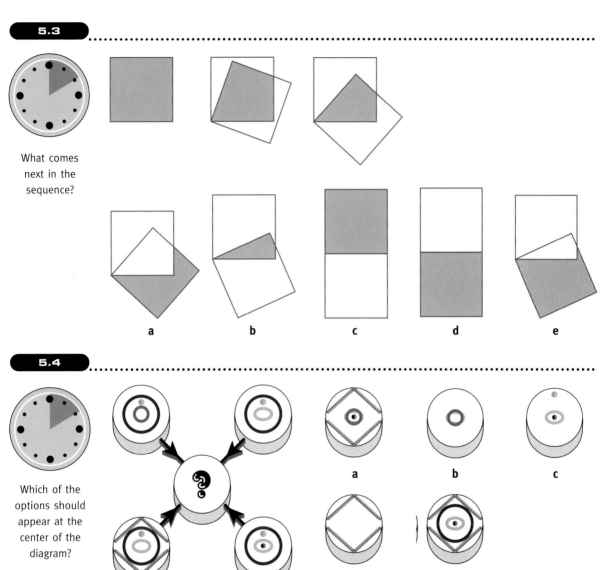

What comes
next in the
sequence?

a   b   c   d   e

5.4

Which of the
options should
appear at the
center of the
diagram?

a   b   c

d   e

Each line and symbol in the four outer circles is transferred to the center circle
according to the following rules: if a line or symbol occurs in the outer circles
once, it is transferred; twice, it is possibly transferred; three times, it is
transferred; four times, it is not transferred.

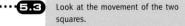

5.3 Look at the movement of the two
squares.

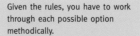

5.4 Given the rules, you have to work
through each possible option
methodically.

For solutions see pages 64-5

Solutions

Workout 1

1.1

A. The red triangle moves to each side of the rectangle clockwise in turn, and alternately flips inside then outside of the rectangle. The blue dot moves counterclockwise to each side of the rectangle in turn, remaining inside the rectangle. The green dot moves clockwise to each side of the rectangle in turn, but is alternately inside and outside of the rectangle.

1.2

D. The circle must appear, eliminating a; the square must appear, eliminating e; the center dot must appear, eliminating b; and c is eliminated because the diagonal line must appear.

1.3

A. The top part, in the first example the red triangle, folds down on top of the line. The bottom part, in the first example the turquoise rectangular figure, folds up behind the line.

1.4

E. Each color moves down its column by one square a time at each stage. A color disappears off the bottom for one stage, reappears at the top of the same column, and recommences its descent.

Workout 2

2.1

B. The brown square, starting on the extreme right, is moving from right to left, one stage at a time.

2.2

A. The colors move as follows:

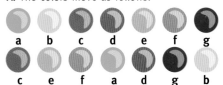

2.3

C. The alternatives are all rotations of the same figure, whereas in option c, the triangle is pointing differently.

2.4

C. An extra triangle is added at each stage on the right. The sequence of colors remains the same from left to right. The dot remains in the left-hand triangle, moving one corner at a time counterclockwise.

Workout 3

3.1

C. At each stage the colors move as follows: red moves three back, two forward; purple moves three forward, two back; yellow moves one back, two forward.

3.2

E. At each stage the counter third from bottom is discarded.

3.3

D. When folded, the blue side with the brown stripe must be next to the orange side with the green stripe, and the brown side with the diagonal red stripe must be on top.

3.4

B. In the example, the top half is folded over on top of the bottom half to make the second figure. Do the same with the third figure.

Workout **4**

4.1

C The orange band rotates through 90°; the ellipse goes on top of the turquoise diamond, which is rotated through 90°. The orange band goes inside the diamond. The green ellipse has rotated through 180°, like the yellow triangle in the first analogy, but it appears the same because of its symmetry.

4.3

A. At each stage, the red arc moves 90° clockwise; the turquoise arc moves 90°; and the blue arc moves 90° counterclockwise.

4.2

C. The yellow circle moves forward and backward between two positions, the blue circle moves 90° clockwise at each stage, the red circle moves backward and forward between two positions, and the green circle moves 90° clockwise at each stage.

4.4

A The blue square turns through 45° clockwise at each stage, and the red diamond folds alternately to the outside, then the inside of the square.

Workout **5**

5.1

E. The ball first appears in the bottom left corner, moves to the bottom right corner, and then the top right corner. As the color sequence is orange, purple, orange, the next color must be purple.

5:3

B. One square remains stationary, the second square gradually rotates in a clockwise direction. The part common to both squares at each stage is shaded yellow.

5.2

E. At each step, the yellow line moves 180°, the orange line moves counterclockwise 120°, the green dot moves counterclockwise 60°, and the brown line moves clockwise 60°.

5.4

A. The turquoise ellipse must be transferred, ruling out d; the green dot is not transferred, ruling out c.
The red circle must be transferred, so only a and b remain. Only a contains the brown lines and the black dot that must be transferred because they only appear once.

Assessment:	
4–6 =	Average
7–10 =	Good
11–14 =	Very good
15–16 =	Exceptional

Sharpen Up Your Memory

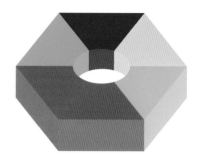

A GOOD MEMORY implies not only skill at memorizing lists of dates and numbers, but also the ability to use memory power efficiently. Recent experiments suggest that we may, in fact, remember everything that happens to us in our lifetime. Large-storage capacity is an important attribute, because the human brain takes in huge amounts of information and processes it all at an incredibly rapid rate. Scientists believe the storage capacity of the brain is sufficient to record a thousand new bits of information every second, from birth to old age – and still have room to spare.

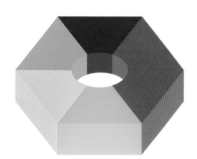

How does one harness this huge brain potential, and what techniques can we adopt in order to improve our memory? Memory devices that enable us to recall important pieces of information include forming associations and the use of mnemonics. While these are all valuable aids to using your memory potential, it is more important to develop your powers of concentration, and to discipline yourself to fix your mind on the subject being studied. The puzzles in this section are designed to develop keenness and clarity of thinking.

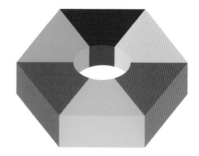

Warming **Up**

The tests in this section are designed to probe all aspects of your memory and, perhaps, to identify areas which you need to work on, starting with short warm-up exercises before progressing further.

1 Study the three automobile license plates for 30 seconds, then cover them and after an interval of 2 minutes answer the questions below.

C 384 AFG

R 291 KLD

B 248 UVH

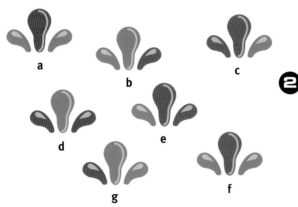

a b c d e f g

2 Study the seven figures for 20 seconds, then cover them and after an interval of 2 minutes answer the questions below.

3 Study these figures and numbers for 20 seconds, then cover them and after an interval of 2 minutes answer the questions below.

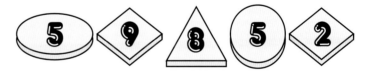

5 9 8 5 2

Questions

1 What color is B 248 UVH?
Complete the license plate R 291 KL.
What color is C 384 AFG?
What color is the middle license plate?
What color is the bottom license plate?

2 Which of the figures appears twice? Describe the color combination.

3 Which figure appears twice?
Which number appears twice?

Workout **1**

These memory exercises are all designed to improve your powers of observation, and ability to retain and recall facts. Study each diagram or picture for the length of time given in the clock face, then cover it, and turn to the opposite page. To check the correct answers, just revert to the original exercises.

1.1

Study this diagram, then cover it, and turn to the opposite page.

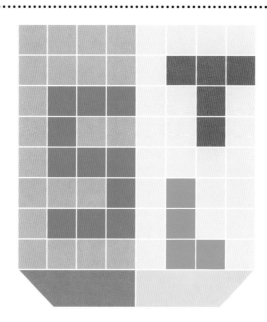

1.2

Study this array of numbers, then cover it, and turn to the opposite page.

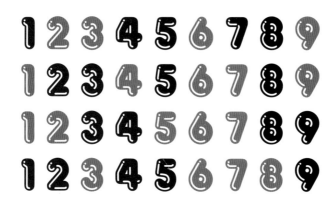

1.1

a What color previously was the number 5?
b What color previously was the letter L?
c What color previously was the letter T?
d What background color previously was
the right-hand side of the square?
e What background color previously was
the left-hand side of the square?

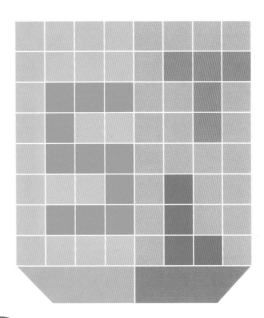

1.2

Which number
is colored red
on every line?

Workout **2**

Study this diagram, then cover it, and turn to the opposite page.

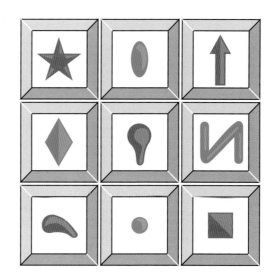

Study this hexagon, then cover it, and turn to the opposite page.

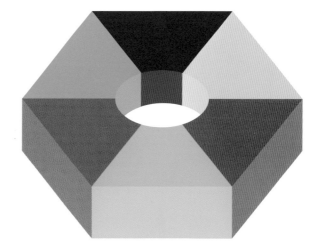

2.1

Which two symbols have changed places?

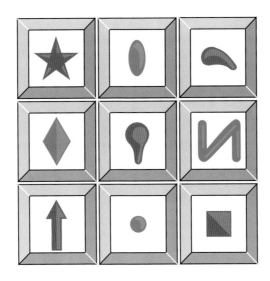

2.2

Which hexagon have you just looked at?

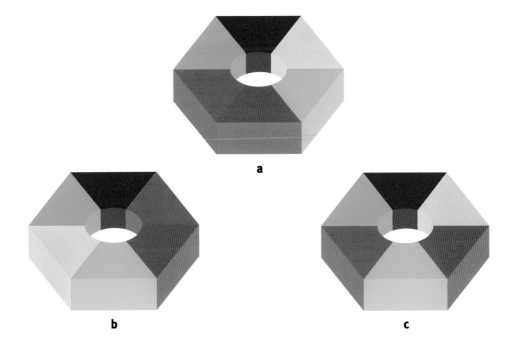

a

b

c

Workout **3**

3.1

Study this grid, then cover it, and turn to the opposite page.

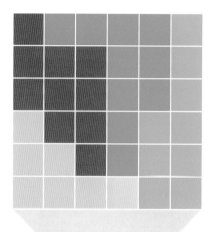

3.2

Study these figures, then cover them, and turn to the opposite page.

   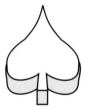

3.1

In what way does this grid differ from the original?

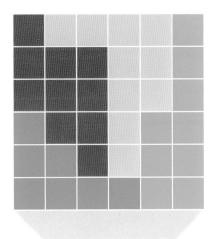

3.2

Which of the following have you just looked at?

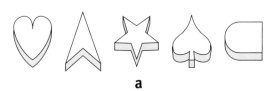

a

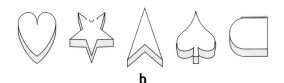

b

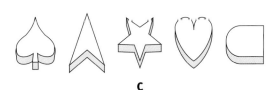

c

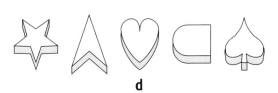

d

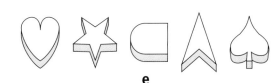

e

Workout **4**

4.1

Study these
letters, then
cover them,
and turn to the
opposite page.

KFGSAOTQUZMERCBF

4.2

Study these
shapes, then
cover them,
and turn to the
opposite page.

4.3

Study this
figure, then
cover it, and
turn to the
opposite page.

4.1

What number is spelled out by the red letters?

4.2

a What letter is inside the triangle?
b What letter is inside the rectangle?
c Which shape contains the letter U?
d What letter is inside the diamond?
e What shape contains the letter I?

4.3

The figure has changed in four ways from the original. List the changes.

Workout **5**

5.1

Study this
matrix of
squares, then
cover it, and
turn to the
opposite page.

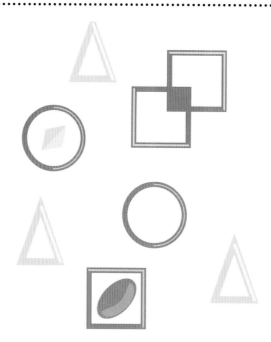

5.2

Study this
figure, then
cover it, and
turn to the
opposite
page.

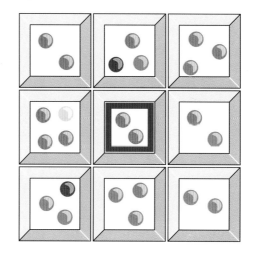

5.1

a   How many green circles appear in total?
b   The square in the middle is surrounded by a border.
    What color is the border?
c   How many red circles appear in each horizontal and
    vertical line of three squares?
d   How many yellow circles appear in total?
e   How many blue circles appear in total?

5.2

a   What color are the two overlapping squares?
b   How many yellow triangles did you see?
c   What color is the ellipse in the green square?
d   What color is the diamond inside one of the circles?
e   How many red triangles did you see?

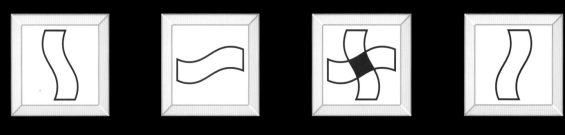

PART 2
THE TESTS

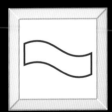 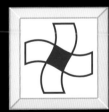  

Don't Panic

ALTHOUGH IT IS EASY to say "Don't panic," when faced with any task or situation that might seem overwhelming at first glance, it is not that easy to do! "Too much to do, and too little time to do it," is a scenario that most of us are faced with frequently, whether at work or when taking an examination. If, however, you have the ability to approach any such circumstance in a logical, calm, and structured fashion, and break down the workload methodically, it is surprising how a task that seems impossible can be made much less daunting.

How can you approach an IQ test confidently and systematically, and without getting into a state of confusion or panic? To start with, it is advisable to carry out some research into the type of questions you may encounter. If the test is a verbal one, there are likely to be questions involving synonyms (a word having the same meaning as another) and antonyms (a word having the opposite meaning to another), questions where you have to find the odd one out, and analogies. Non-verbal tests also include analogies – a multitude of relations where you must reason out the answer from a parallel case – and odd ones out (classification), where it is necessary to find the one case that does not fit in a number of options.

On beginning the test, make sure that you read through every question quickly, because it is vital to understand the instructions and exactly what is required. In a timed test, start by doing all the questions where the answer hits you immediately. Then do all the ones that can be solved with just a little thought, and finally the ones that take up the most time. When faced with multiple-choice tests, make sure that you answer every one of them, even if you are short of time. It is very unlikely that you will guess all of them wrongly, especially if you follow your intuition.

If it is allowed, have plenty of extra paper available for making notes or doing calculations. When faced with a set of diagrams, first try to decide what logical patterns and/or sequences are occurring, and then look at the options to see if one fits in with your pattern of thought. If you have time to spare at the end of the test, don't just sit back with an air of satisfaction, but rather

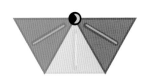

utilize the extra time to have a quick review of your answers. We all have been guilty of slips of the pen at one time or another, and this may just be one of those occasions.

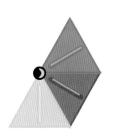

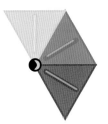

Last, but not least, try to be in the right frame of mind. It is likely that you will have some anxiety symptoms prior to taking any kind of test; these are often called "butterflies in the stomach." Psychological studies have shown that a certain degree of anxiety can be helpful in a test situation,

because it shows that you are concentrating on the job. On the other hand, if you are overly anxious, this is likely to affect your performance adversely. If you are feeling harassed or upset by some personal issue, try to put it temporarily to the back of your mind. Above all, look to relax and focus your mind on the task before you in an analytical way.

The **Tests**

Check your progress and assess your performance with this special test section.
Each of the two tests consists of 25 questions; each is of a similar degree of difficulty, and includes
a selection of the types of puzzles encountered in the previous chapters. The time limit for each
test is 60 minutes – any delay will invalidate your score, so work as quickly as possible.
A performance assessment is provided with the solutions on pages 104–9.

Test **1** – 60 **minutes**

1.1

Which of the circles below should replace the question mark?

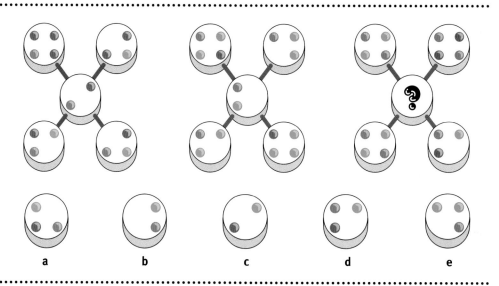

| a | b | c | d | e |

1.2

Which number is twice as many as the number immediately to the left of the number that is two squares below the number that lies midway between the lowest even number in the grid and the number in the square immediately below the highest odd number?

22	62	6	11	15	57
28	13	36	8	27	16
3	17	24	38	12	64
72	30	10	4	46	34
20	5	68	18	7	25
9	78	26	56	14	70

1.3

Look at the grid of numbers
in question 1.2 for 10 seconds,
then turn immediately to
page 91.

1.4

Which is the
odd one out?

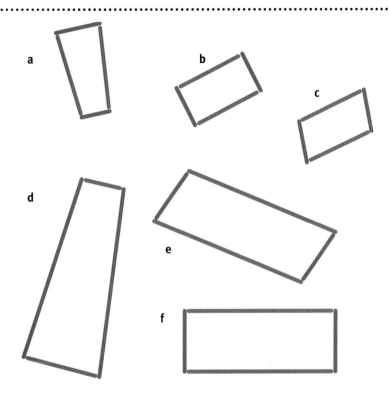

a

b

c

d

e

f

1.5

What is the
missing number?

1.6

Which section should replace the section in the circle that is not colored?

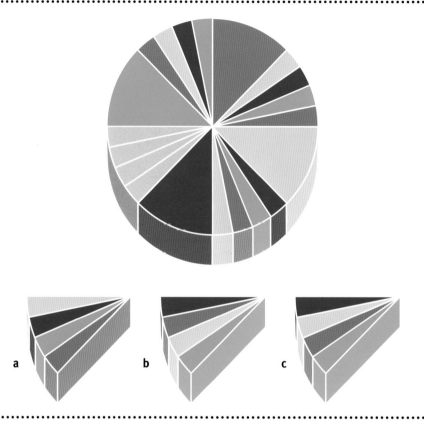

a

b

c

1.7

What number continues this sequence?

7, 13, 8.5, 10.5, 10, 8, ?

1.8

How much money does Al have?

Al has $6 more than Bill, but if Bill had three times more than he has now, he would have $6 more than the combined original amounts of money.

1.9

Which of the five boxes below is most like the box above?

a   b   c   d   e

1.10

Which figure continues the sequence?

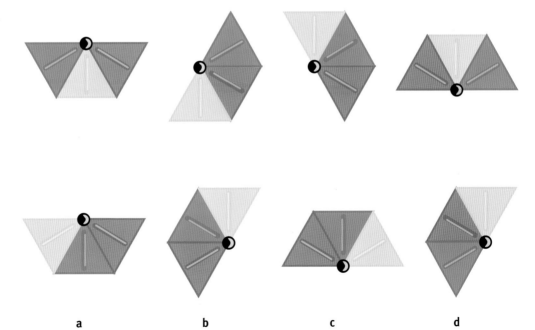

a   b   c   d

1.11

What number should replace the question mark?

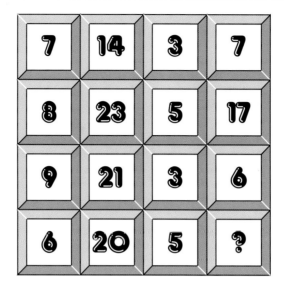

1.12

Which is the missing tile?

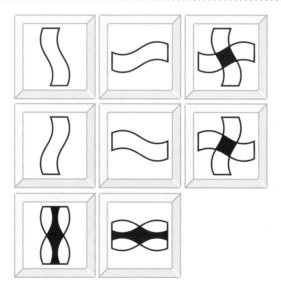

   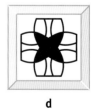

a   b   c   d

1.13

What are the chances that at least one of the balls will be black?

Imagine two bags. Each bag contains eight balls, four white balls and four black balls. A ball is drawn out of bag one, and another ball out of bag two.

a 1 in 4

b 1 in 2

c 2 in 3

d 3 in 4

1.14

Study this diagram for 25 seconds, then turn to page 91.

1.15

What comes next in the sequence?

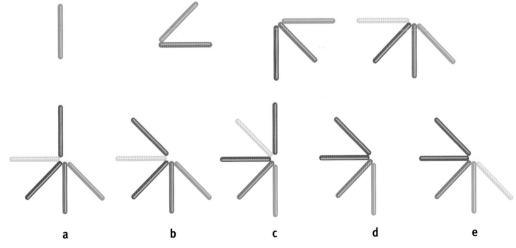

a b c d e

1.16

What number should replace the question mark?

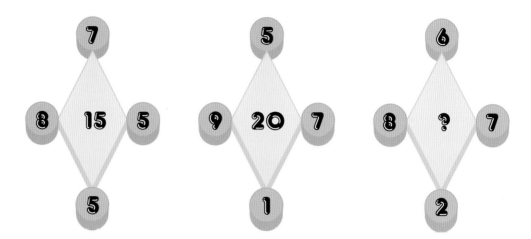

1.17

Which is the odd one out?

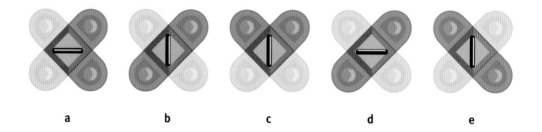

a   b   c   d   e

1.18

Only one person told the truth. Who broke the cup?

Four children were in the kitchen, with a broken cup on the floor.
"Philip did it," said Charlie
"William broke it," said Philip.
"It wasn't me," said Ken.
"Philip is a liar when he said I did it," said William.

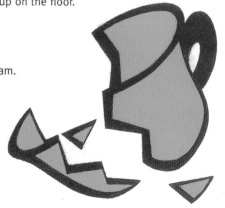

1.19

How can you remove two of the toothpicks to leave only three squares?

Eight toothpicks have been arranged to make a total of fourteen squares, that is one very large square, four medium-size squares and nine small squares.

1.20

Work out the following relationship.

is to:

as

is to:

?

a

b

c

d

e

1.21

Which two three-digit numbers come next in the sequence?

202, 122, 232, 425, 262, 728, ?, ?

1.22

What continues the sequence?

a

b

c

d

e

1.23

What number should replace the question mark?

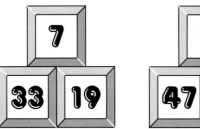

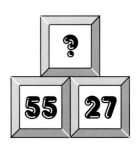

1.24

Which is the
odd one out?

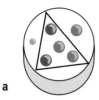 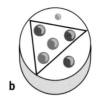 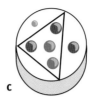 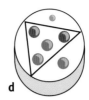

a   b   c   d

e   f   g

1.25

Which number
is the odd one
out?

a   763236

b   817182

c   384615

d   217872

e   436563

Questions 1.3 and 1.14

1.3

What number is in the bottom right-hand corner?

1.14

Which two
symbols have
changed places?

Test 2 – 60 minutes

2.1

Work out the following relationship.

is to:

as

is to:

?

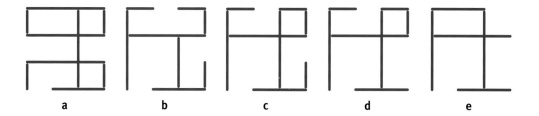

a   b   c   d   e

2.2

How many days had the workman worked?

A workman receives $20 for each day that he works, but forfeits $30 for each day that he doesn't work under the terms of his contract. After 30 days he finds that he has forfeited as much money as he has earned.

2.3

Which of the following continues the sequence?

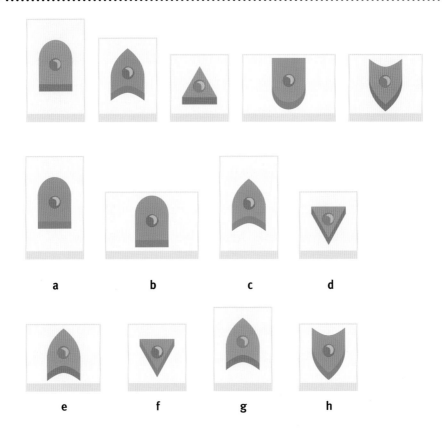

a b c d

e f g h

2.4

What is the total of the five faces indicated, that is, the four faces where the dice rest on each other and the very bottom face?

Three standard dice are stacked one on top of the other. We can see that the very top face is 4.

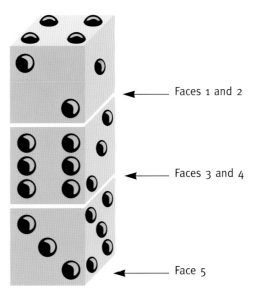

Faces 1 and 2

Faces 3 and 4

Face 5

2.5

Work out the following time relationship.

How many minutes is it before midnight if 1½ hours ago it was twice as many minutes past 8 P.M.?

2.6

Which hexagon continues the sequence?

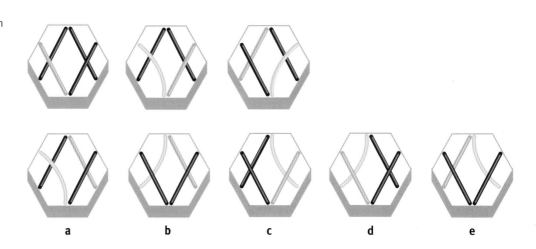

a   b   c   d   e

2.7

Study these faces for 10 seconds, then turn to page 103.

2.8

How can you move only four toothpicks to new positions to produce three identical squares?

These twelve toothpicks have been arranged to produce five squares, one large and four small ones.

2.9

How old am I now?

The age of my son is the same as the digits of my age reversed. A year ago I was twice the age of my son.

2.10

When this is folded to form a cube, just one of the following can be produced. Which one?

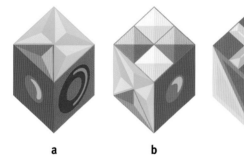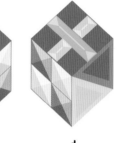

a   b   c   d   e

2.11

Look at the plan of the cube in question 2.10 for 20 seconds, then turn to page 103.

2.12

Which is the
missing circle?

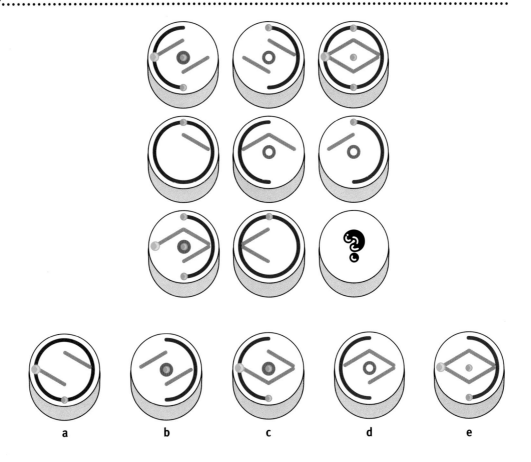

a   b   c   d   e

2.13

What number
should replace
the question
mark?

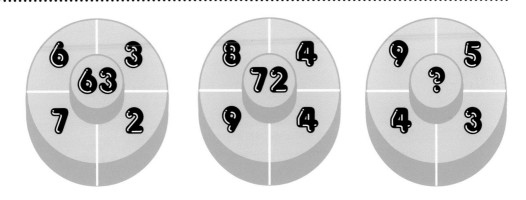

2.14

Can you list the eight squares of paper in the correct order, from the top sheet down to the bottom sheet?

Eight square pieces of paper, all exactly the same size, have been placed on top of one another, overlapping as shown.

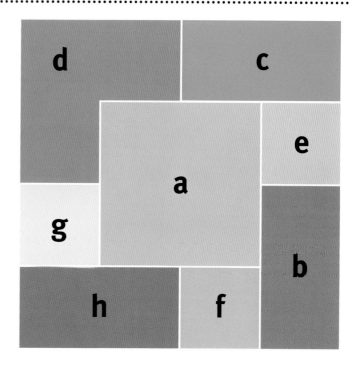

2.15

Which is the missing section?

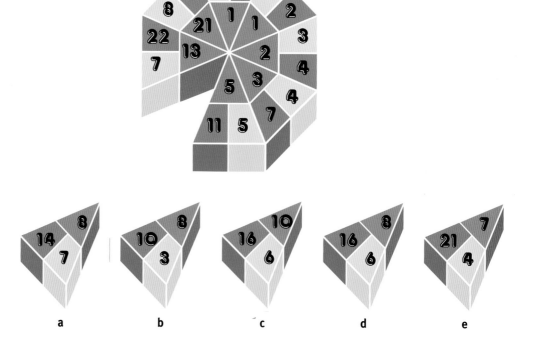

2.16

Four of these pieces can be fitted together to form a perfect square. Which is the odd one out?

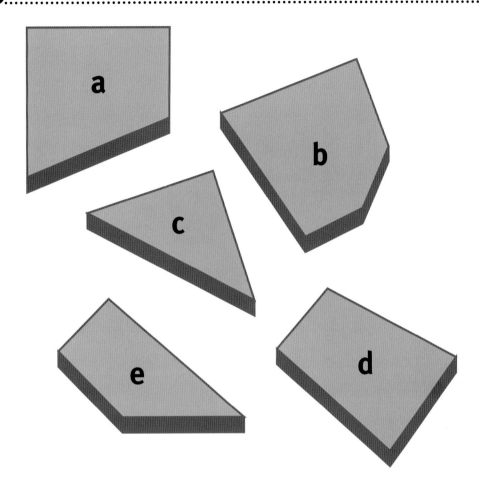

2.17

What comes next in the sequence?

0, 1, – 1, 0, – 2, ?

2.18

Which of the five boxes below is most like the box on the right?

a   b   c   d   e

2.19

What number should replace the question mark?

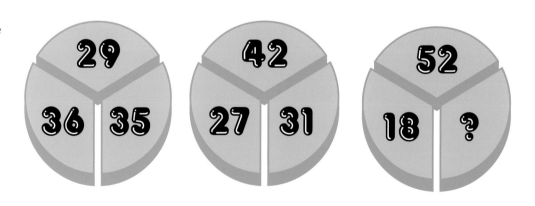

2.20

What is the speed of the faster car?

A car travels 80 miles (treat as km) in the time that another car, traveling 10 mph (treat as kmph) faster, travels 100 miles (km).

2.21

What comes next in this sequence?

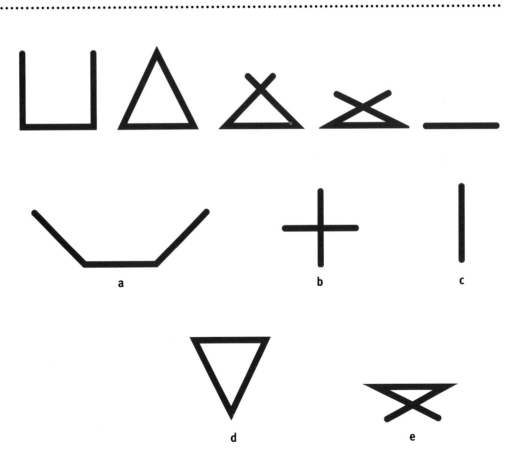

a

b

c

d

e

2.22

Which is the odd one out?

a   b   c   d   e

2.23

Which set of numbers below has the same relationship to each other as the numbers above?

2846 : 642 : 24

a   3821 : 321 : 15

b   6849 : 948 : 49

c   7296 : 627 : 26

d   3619 : 913 : 13

e   9876 : 427 : 56

2.24

Which of the shapes below comes next in the sequence?

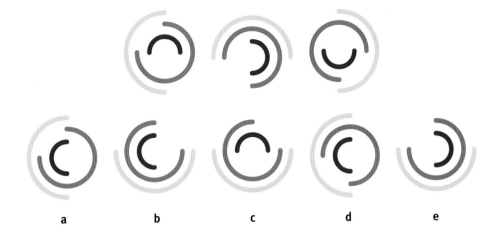

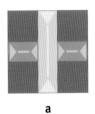

a   b   c   d   e

2.25

What comes next in the sequence?

574, 628, 696, 762, ?

Questions 2.7 and 2.11

2.7

One of the faces was different from the rest. Which of these was it?

2.11

Which of these figures appears on one side of the cube?

a   b   c   d

Solutions Test 1

1.1

B. A dot is transferred to the middle circle only after it has appeared in the outer circles in the same position three times.

1.2

The answer is 36.

1.3

The answer is 70.

1.4

D. The two longest sides are purple. In all the others, the two shortest sides are purple.

1.5

1. Start at 11 and jump two segments at a time working clockwise, deducting 1, then 2, then 3 and finally 4.

1.6

C. Starting at a red segment and working clockwise, the color sequence of segments, irrespective of size, is red, yellow, blue, green.

1.7

11.5. There are two alternate series: 7, 8.5, 10, 11.5 (that is + 1.5) and 13, 10.5, 8, 5.5 (that is − 2.5).

1.8

$18. Al: $18, Bill: $12 (A + B = $30) × 3 = $36.

1.9

E. The red segment is in just two circles.

1.10

D. Each triangle takes it in turn to flip around clockwise on a central pivot. First the blue triangle flips around, then yellow, then red, and finally blue again.

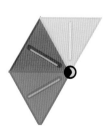

1.11

10. Reading across each line:

$(7 \times 3) - 14 = 7$
$(8 \times 5) - 23 = 17$
$(9 \times 3) - 21 = 6$

therefore $(6 \times 5) - 20 = 10$.

1.12

C. Looking across each line and down each column, the contents of the third square are formed by merging the contents of the first two. Only the portion common to the merging of the first two figures is colored blue in the final square.

1.13

D. The possible combinations of drawing the balls are black-black, white-white, black-white and white-black – the only one of the four possible combinations where black does not occur is white-white. The chances of drawing at least one black ball are, therefore, three chances in four.

1.14

The answer is bell and star.

1.15

C. At each stage, working clockwise, another colored arm is added and each colored arm rotates 45° clockwise.

1.16

The answer is 19: $(6 + 8 + 7) - 2$.

1.17

B. Options a and c are the same figure rotated, and options d and e are the same figure rotated.

1.18

The answer is Ken.

GUILTY	SPOKEN BY	TRUE OR FALSE
Charlie	Ken and William	False
William	Ken and Philip	False
Philip	Ken and Charlie	False
Ken	William	True

1.19

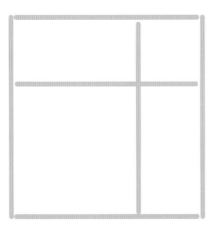

1.20

C. The top figure is folded down along the dividing line on top of the bottom figure.

1.21

293, 031. If you change the spacing you get: 20, 21, 22, 23, 24, 25, 26, 27, 28, 29, 30, 31.

1.22

E. Orange moves one left, two right; blue moves one left, one right; yellow moves two right, one left; turquoise moves one left, two right.

1.23

The answer is 14: $(55 - 27) \div 2$.

1.24

E. Option a is the same figure as d rotated, option c is the same figure as b rotated, and option f is the same figure as g rotated.

1.25

D. In the other options, the two halves total 999, that is $763 + 236$.

Solutions Test **2**

2.1

C. The two are added together to make a square grid:

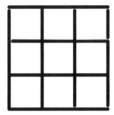

2.2

He has worked for 18 days (18 × 20 = $360), but has not worked for 12 days (12 × 30 = $360).

2.3

F. The three rectangles are repeated, but lie horizontal instead of vertical. The three internal figures are also repeated, but rotate through 180°. The color of the dot alternates blue/red, and the color of the internal figure alternates red/blue.

2.4

17. Because opposite sides of a die always total 7, the bottom face of the top die must be 3 (that is 7 − 4). Face 2 plus face 3 must total 7, and face four plus face five must total 7. The total of all 5 faces is, therefore, 7 + 7 + 3 = 17.

2.5

The answer is 50 minutes.

2.6

B. Each line is colored red in turn. After it has been colored red it appears as a curved yellow line in the next option only.

2.7

The answer is 8: (3 + 5).

2.8

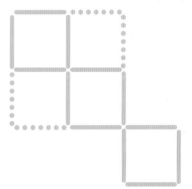

2.9

The answer is 73.

2.10

The answer is b.

2.11

The answer is c.

2.12

C. Looking both across and down, the contents of the third circle are formed by adding together the contents of the first two circles, except that similar symbols disappear.

2.13

The answer is 60: (5 × 4) × (9 ÷ 3).

2.14

The order is a, d, g, h, f, b, e, and c.

2.15

D. Within the octagon there are three separate sequences: the yellow sequence runs 1, 2, 3, 4, 5, 6, 7, 8; the blue sequence runs 1, 2, 4, 7, 11, 16, 22, 29, that is + 1, + 2, + 3, etc.; the red sequence runs 1, 1, 2, 3, 5, 8, 13, 21, that is each number is produced by adding together the previous two.

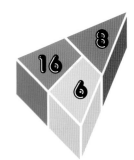

2.16

The answer is a.

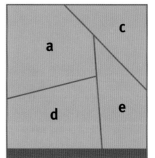

2.17

− **1.** There are two separate sequences both deducting 1 each time, that is: 0, − 1, − 2 and 1, 0, − 1.

2.18

C. One red dot appears in the square only, and one red dot appears both in the circle and square.

2.19

30. The three numbers in each circle add up to 100.

2.20

The answer is 50 mph (treat as kmph).

2.21

E. The two arms that start in the vertical position move clockwise and counterclockwise respectively at an equal rate at each stage.

2.22

E. Options a and d have red/blue reversal, and so have options b and c.

2.23

C. Each number is the previous number reversed, with the omission of the highest digit.

2.24

B. At each stage, the yellow arc moves 90° clockwise; the red arc moves 90° counterclockwise; and the blue arc moves 90° clockwise.

2.25

834. Add the number formed by the first and last digits at each stage, that is 762 + 72 = 834.

Assessment:

10-12 = Average
13-15 = Good
16-19 = Very good
20-22 = Excellent
23-24 = Exceptional
25 = Amazing!

INDEX

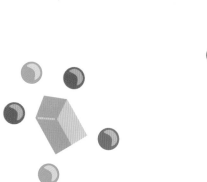

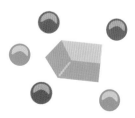

112

FURTHER READING

Alpha Group.
The Complete Idiot's Guide to Improving Your IQ.
Topanga: AlphaBooks, 1999.

Carter, Philip J. and Kenneth A. Russell.
Challenging IQ Tests.
New York: Sterling Publications, 1998.

Carter, Philip J. and Kenneth A. Russell.
IQ Powerplay: Can You Do It.
Toronto: McClelland & Stewart, 1995.

Eysenck, H. J.
Test Your IQ.
New York: Penguin USA, 1995.

Makintosh, N. J.,
IQ and Human Intelligence.
New York: Oxford University Press, 1998.

Murphy, Emmett C.
Leadership IQ.
New York: John Wiley & Sons, 1997.

Perkins, David.
Outsmarting IQ: The Emerging Science of Learnable Intelligence.
New York: Free Press, 1995.

Seligman, Daniel.
A Question of Intelligence: The IQ Debate in America.
Secaucus: Citadel Press, 1994

Sternberg, Robert J. and Patricia Ruzgis.
Personality and Intelligence.
New York: Cambridge University Press, 1994.

Winter, Arthur and Ruth Winter.
Brain Workout: Easy Ways to Power Up Your Memory, Sensory Perception, and Intelligence.
New York: St. Martin's Press, 1997.

Index by Mary Norris